Original title:
The Forest Fable

Copyright © 2025 Creative Arts Management OÜ
All rights reserved.

Author: Theodore Sinclair
ISBN HARDBACK: 978-1-80567-046-9
ISBN PAPERBACK: 978-1-80567-126-8

The Eulogy of Autumn Leaves

Once bright and bold in lively trees,
They dance away with the autumn breeze.
Adieu, dear leaves, your time's now past,
You've joined the ground in a leafy cast.

We'll miss your colors, vibrant and bright,
You flapped like banners in morning light.
Now crunched beneath our carefree feet,
A crispy chorus, a rustling beat.

With a giddy twirl, you laugh and dive,
A final jig before you arrive.
In piles and mounds, you gather 'round,
Who knew demise could be so sound?

So here's to you, oh leaves of gold,
In your crisp embrace, new stories unfold.
Let's raise a cup to your funny plight,
For even in falling, you took to flight.

The Treetop Troubadours

High above in the swaying trees,
Singing squirrels entertain with ease.
With acorn drums and twiggy guitars,
They serenade all the passing cars.

The branches sway to their wild refrain,
A jolly tune after summer's reign.
Singing loudly, without a care,
The woodlands echo their playful air.

A raccoon joins with a croaky chant,
The audience flies in, a curious ant.
Birds tap their feet, trying to keep pace,
While bees buzz around in a fuzzy race.

With pines for stage and clouds above,
These treetop stars share tunes of love.
A whimsical show, no tickets sold,
Just laughter-filled moments, pure joy to uphold.

Portraits of the Quiet Wood

In a grove where whispers play,
Trees pose proudly throughout the day.
Each knot and gnarled branch may seem bland,
But they hold secrets, as only they can.

The owls roll their eyes at passing folks,
While raccoons snicker at silly jokes.
"Why did the squirrel bring a ladder?" they quip,
"To reach the nuts on the high-flying trip!"

Sunlight dapples with a soft embrace,
As shadows pirouette with midair grace.
Each flower chuckles, adorned in bloom,
Painting the earth with joyful perfume.

So stroll through this canvas, nature's delight,
Where laughter lingers in morning light.
Among the branches, let yourself roam,
In quiet woods, you'll find a home.

Glimmers of Hope in Glistening Dew

In the morning light they play,
Dewdrops dance in a joyous sway.
Squirrels giggle, chasing their tails,
While a snail dreams of grand fairy tales.

A robin hops, with worms in sight,
Looking quite chubby, what a delight!
With each chirp, a silly joke,
Among the trees, laughter awoke.

A Tapestry of Shadows and Sunlight.

Under branches, the shadows creep,
Where wise old owls have secrets to keep.
A bear in shades reads maps upside down,
While rabbits play dress-up in goofy crowns.

The sunbeams wink, it's a funny scene,
With dancing leaves and a playful dream.
A gathering of critters, all so spry,
They plan a parade with a wink and a shy.

Whispers Among Trees

The trees gossip in rustling tones,
About the antics of wild jokey clones.
A hedgehog once claimed he could outrun,
A snail who thought he was quite the fun!

Frogs dressed in ties, croak out their tunes,
While fireflies twinkle like bright little moons.
A raccoon with shades talks big game,
But trips on his feet, oh what a shame!

Echoes of the Canopy

Echoes bounce off branches wide,
Tickling fawns who cannot hide.
The woodpecker makes a drumming beat,
As chipmunks gather for a snack to eat.

In bushes, butterflies play tag,
While hedgehogs ponder, looking rather drag.
A chorus of laughter, sweet and bright,
Makes the sunlight giggle, what a sight!

Guardians of the Green

In the woods where squirrels prance,
The mushrooms dance, they take a chance.
A fox in boots, a bunny grand,
They're all together, a merry band.

With acorn hats and twiggy swords,
They plot their schemes in whispered words.
"Shall we steal the owl's bright hat?"
They giggle, echoing, "Just like that!"

The trees all chuckle, leaves in cheer,
As rabbits hop and draw them near.
The guardian crew of leafy blends,
With laughter and joy, their fun never ends.

Reverie in the Woodland Shadows

Beneath the boughs, a shadow plays,
Where raccoons host their nightly frays.
They dip and dive, in moonlit beams,
In search of snacks, or so it seems.

A bear in pajamas, snoring loud,
In slumber dreams with a cuddly crowd.
The fireflies blink, a party's begun,
With woodland creatures, oh what fun!

The owls hoot tunes, from high up above,
Sprinkling the night with whispers of love.
A jam session blooms, each critter groovy,
In shadows they dance, moves oh so smoothy.

The Music of Timbered Tranquility

In the forest where echoes ring,
The birds compose a cheerful zing.
A woodpecker drumming a cheery beat,
Makes the downy babies dance on their feet.

The deer strut by, in stylish flair,
While raccoons prepare a grand carnival fair.
The trees sway low, in rhythm, they lean,
As trunks tickle branches, a sight so serene.

The breeze hums tunes like a playful child,
Nature's orchestra, sweet and wild.
With giggles and chirps, the concert fills,
A symphony born from babbling rills.

Legends from the Leafy Depths

Once in the glade, a story grew,
Of rabbits that wore capes, who knew what to do.
They'd save the day with carrots in hand,
A heroic team, a veggie-bound band.

But one little hare had a tale to tell,
Of a squirrel who slipped and fell in a well.
With laughter that echoed, it spread like fire,
A legend born from a slip-up so dire.

The word spread fast, through the frisky pack,
Now tales and giggles bounce off the track.
In leafy depths, their stories thrive,
Guardians of humor, yes, they're alive!

Tales Beneath the Boughs

A squirrel dressed in a tiny hat,
Pranced around like a chatty brat.
He danced with glee to a song so sweet,
While stealing acorns, oh, quite the cheat.

The wise old owl wore glasses round,
Reading volumes on the forest ground.
With every turn of a leaf or twig,
He'd chuckle softly, oh, how he'd dig.

A rabbit hopped with shoes of lace,
In a bouncing race, he'd set the pace.
But tripped on roots, fell with a thud,
And landed right in a muddy flood.

The raccoons held a nighttime feast,\nWith berries and bread, it was quite the beast.
They laughed and snacked till the moonlight waned,\nAwake 'til dawn, their laughter uncontained.

Secrets of the Sylvan Realm

Among the trees, a turtle raced,
His shell painted bright, a winning face.
But oh, so slow, he aimed to boast,
While the rabbits giggled, he'd never coast.

A hedgehog wore a spiky crown,
Claiming he'd rule the woodland town.
But in a gust, his hat blew far,
And off he scrambled, what a bizarre star!

A fox in shades gave a wise old nod,
Claiming to know the path to God.
Yet lost in brambles, he spun around,
And ended up where he'd first been found.

The badger built a rickety slide,
For critters to ride with joy and pride.
But when they soared, the thing would crash,
Creating a spectacle, a comical splash!

Shadows of the Timberland

In shadows deep, the critters play,
A stag in sneakers hopped all day.
With every leap, he'd strike a pose,
And give a wink, oh, how he chose.

The raccoon played a sneaky game,
Turning night into wild, full flame.
He swiped a pizza from a campsite,
And danced 'round fires, what a delight!

A bear with clumsy ballet shoes,
Practiced pirouettes, gave snoopy snooze.
He twirled and spun, tripped on his back,
The forest roared with laughter, what a knack!

The shadows whispered, trees would hum,
Of all the fun, it was never glum.
They whispered tales of silly quests,
And under the moon, they took their rests.

The Chronicles of Moss and Moonlight

When dusk arrived, the crickets sang,
A mole on stage, took a grand pang.
With tiny paws, he played the drum,
And all around, the forest would hum.

An ant with shades led a parade,
As tiny confetti serenely swayed.
They marched through leaves, on paths unseen,
In joyous chatter, a big machine!

The fireflies twinkled, lights aglow,
While dancing frogs put on a show.
In bows and tutus, they leap and glide,
A laughter fest, no place to hide.

And as the stars blinked bright above,
The forest echoed with glee and love.
For in this realm of spark and cheer,
Each night was grand, year after year.

Illuminated Trails

Beneath the moon's bright grin,
The fireflies throw their light,
A squirrel stays up too late,
With acorns stacked just right.

He starts to play a tune,
On a leaf that's shaped like a drum,
His friends join in a chorus,
With a giggle and a hum.

The owl hoots in confusion,
Wondering what's that sound?
A party in the treetops,
Where laughter can be found.

So when the sun starts rising,
The woodland still can see,
A trail of funny stories,
From squirrels wild and free.

The Gathering of the Woodland Creatures

In the glade where laughter sips,
The animals gather round,
A rabbit boasts of jumping tricks,
While others cheer the sound.

The badger brings some snacks,
A berry pie that's very sweet,
But the raccoon sneaks a taste,
Claiming it's a special treat!

The deer shows off her moves,
While twirling in the dew,
And all the critters laugh out loud,
For nothing else will do.

As twilight dims the scene,
They share their tales with glee,
And the woods echo with laughter,
In their whimsical decree.

Forgotten Myths of the Thicket

Old tales told by the trees,
Of giants made of muck,
Who danced with every breeze,
And all they did was cluck.

A hedgehog heard them whisper,
And thought he'd join the fun,
He gathered up his courage,
To dance until he's spun.

But all the birds took flight,
At the sight of prickly fears,
And the stories turned to giggles,
As they caught their honest tears.

So if you roam the thicket,
Listen to the leaves,
You might find those funny tales,
Woven in the eaves.

The Dance of Fern and Fern

Two ferns with feathery fronds,
Decide to start a dance,
They sway and twirl with grace,
And give the breeze a chance.

The mossy floor holds back,
As mushrooms try to peek,
While beetles clap their tiny hands,
In rhythm, not so sleek.

But as they jig and wiggle,
A snort comes from nearby,
A piglet walks in curious,
To know just what's awry.

So the ferns just laugh it off,
And show him how to sway,
And soon the woods have joined the fun,
For dancing's here to stay.

Legends Woven in Wood

In the trees, squirrels plot,
With acorns as their gold,
Rabbits dance in wild design,
And owls just watch, so bold.

Bears wear hats, quite dapper too,
Strutting through the glade,
While deer laugh at their fumbles,
In the merry promenade.

The ants march on in lines so straight,
With tiny flags held high,
Each grain of sugar, a victory,
Underneath the sunny sky.

And at dusk, the crickets sing,
Tales of silly quests,
While fireflies twinkle like stars,
In this woodland game of jest.

The Symphony of Woodland Harmony

The raccoons form a band at night,
With cans as drums, they play,
While frogs hop in, with croaking tunes,
To liven up the fray.

A bear with shades in sunny spots,
Sips honey from a jar,
While mice hold tight to paper kites,
And giggle from afar.

The trees sway gently, keep the beat,
As critters leap and prance,
Nature's joke, a wild concert,
In every leaf's great dance.

And though the night may seem quite calm,
A hoot or chitter's heard,
For each creature knows its part here,
In the symphony absurd.

Fables of the Rooted Spirits

Underneath the towering pines,
The gnomes tell tales at dusk,
Of leaping frogs and changing winds,
With notes of earthy musk.

The spiders weave their webs with glee,
While ants perform ballet,
The mushrooms cheer from little seats,
As twilight steals the day.

Wise old trees hold secrets deep,
And chuckle as they sway,
For every root has got a joke,
That makes the branches play.

The owls wink down encouragingly,
On tales that make you grin,
With spirits grounded, rooted deep,
Let the laughter begin.

Constellations of the Woodland Sky

At night, the stars have curious shapes,
Like squirrels in a race,
While clouds drift by, a fluffy crew,
In this cosmic chase.

The fireflies flicker, flash, and wink,
Their dance a glowing sight,
As raccoons point to shapes above,
In whispers full of light.

A badger snickers at the moon,
Saying it's quite round,
While owls share their wisdom here,
In this forest playground.

Every twinkle is a story,
Of critters on the fly,
In constellations, laughter blooms,
Beneath the endless sky.

Enchanted Glades

In a glade where rabbits dance,
Squirrels try their funny prance.
A deer with shades and swanky flair,
Claims he's the best with fancy hair.

A wise old owl gives a hoot,
Tells tales of a sneaky root.
That trips the ants when they march by,
And makes them all but tumble dry.

Leaves giggle in the gentle breeze,
While buzzards tease the bumblebees.
They try to take a honey dip,
But end up in a sticky trip.

The sun breaks through, the shadows play,
The forest giggles all the day.
With every critter, laugh's a must,
In enchanted glades of joyful trust.

Stories Nestled in the Underbrush

In the underbrush, tales are spun,
Of raccoons who just can't run.
Chasing tails of their own kind,
Always leaving laughter behind.

A hedgehog wore a tiny hat,
Declared he was the king of that.
But when he rolled, oh what a sight,
The hat flew off into the night.

The bushes rustle, whispers dance,
As bunnies start a silly prance.
They throw a party near the brook,
With nutty snacks and a storybook.

Each critter shares their wildest dream,
In fables where the giggles stream.
Under the stars, they gather 'round,
With joyful stories, laughter's found.

Ballad of the Bark and Leaf

In the grove where branches sway,
Bark and leaf have much to say.
Tree trunks wear their best disguise,
As leafy arms wave, oh so spry.

A chipmunk starts to sing a tune,
While dancing 'neath the glowing moon.
He's got moves that make you laugh,
A comedic little acrobat graph.

The rusty wind begins to tease,
Whispering jokes to wobbly trees.
The squirrels snicker, running fast,
While branches sway and shadows cast.

And every creature joins the fun,
In this bark and leaf court jest run.
They laugh 'til dawn, the sun peeks bright,
In a wild, whimsical forest light.

The Hidden Grove's Lore

In a grove that's tucked away,
Frogs tell jokes to brighten day.
With gassy croaks, they share a laugh,
Their ribbits serving as a graph.

A beaver builds a silly dam,
But ends up stuck—oh what a jam!
He winks and waves, a true delight,
While fish swim by and giggle, right?

The bumblebee spins tales of woe,
When pollen's lost in blossoms' glow.
He buzzes loud but can't find home,
Yet chuckles as he starts to roam.

Under the shade, they gather near,
In hidden grooves, there's naught to fear.
With tales galore and laughter free,
Such is the lore of joy, you see!

Reflections on the Twilit Trail

In the twilight, shadows prance,
Squirrels wear a silly stance.
Talking trees with grumpy faces,
Plotting tricks in hidden places.

Bunnies hop and start a race,
While hedgehogs play a quiet bass.
A wise old owl spills some tea,
Laughing at the history.

Fireflies dance in brilliant swirls,
While raccoons plot to steal some pearls.
The moon chuckles, shines so bright,
As critters scheme all through the night.

Parables of the Nestled Nook

In a nook, the gnomes convene,
Crafting hats like seen in dreams.
Their leader stumbles, falls from grace,
Bumps his head—oh, what a face!

Bunnies gather, snacks in paws,
Sharing tales with grand applause.
A turtle slow, with witty charm,
Steals the show, but means no harm.

A pixie darts, her wings ablaze,
In the chaos, all just gaze.
With laughter ringing through the trees,
The gnomes agree, this brings them ease.

Fables Carved in Twisted Trunks

Twisted trunks tell tales so grand,
Of raccoons who form a band.
They drum on logs and sing their song,
Confusing foxes all night long.

Chipmunks join, they bring the cheer,
With tiny shouts that all can hear.
Their dance is wild, a quirky sight,
While owls hoot at the silly night.

A beaver tries to dance along,
Trips on roots, oh, how he's wrong!
Yet laughter echoes through the glade,
These tales of fun will never fade.

The Lament of the Forgotten Thicket

In the thicket, dreams once soared,
Now only crickets seem bored.
A hedgehog sighs, his heart's now full,
As chubby rabbits play it cool.

Frogs croak tales of glory passed,
Once they raced, but now it's fast.
They reminisce of youthful grit,
While munching bugs and taking a sit.

A thistle sways, holds memories tight,
Tales of ruckus in the night.
Yet still they smile, a joyous huddle,
For every tale has a bit of muddle.

The Parchment of Petals

In a world of blooming cheer,
A flower claimed to be a seer.
It whispered secrets, oh so sweet,
But tangled roots caused funny feet.

The bees would laugh as they flew by,
While petals danced, oh so spry.
Each breeze gave giggles, soft and bright,
As blossoms twinkled in delight.

A squirrel tried to take a nap,
On a cushion made of flower map.
But every time he closed his eyes,
A petal tickled—oh, what a surprise!

So in this garden, joy was found,
With chuckles ringing all around.
Nature's laughter filled the air,
A silly tale without a care.

Carved in Cedar

A tree once carved with funny signs,
Declared it loved the sun, not vines.
The animals paused, they laughed aloud,
'You're just a trunk, not very proud!'

A wise old owl perched on a limb,
Said, 'Cedar, dear, don't be so dim.'
For every mark is a chance to joke,
Even a tree can be a poke!

From squirrels to owls and even fox,
They gathered 'round, all in one box.
They painted faces on the bark,
Creating mischief in the dark.

And when the moon shone on the scene,
They danced and sang as if a dream,
Underneath the cedar's grins,
Nature's laughter surely wins.

Alchemy of the Woodland Heart

In the woods where joy collides,
A wizard stirs while humor guides.
He mixed laughter with the dew,
And magic sprouted, oh it grew!

The mushrooms giggled, round and stout,
As bunnies hopped and twirled about.
The trees would chuckle, leaves a-flutter,
Every time they saw a butter.

A single acorn tried to sing,
But only made a funny ping.
The woodland creatures, tickled pink,
Joined in laughter with a wink.

And so they danced all through the night,
Under the stars, a charming sight.
For in this wood of mirth and glee,
Every heart beats joyfully.

The Portal of Pine and Peace

A portal made of pine so tall,
Invited creatures, one and all.
With every step, they'd trip and stumble,
The forest echoed, laughter rumbled.

A hedgehog thought he'd glide right through,
But got stuck, oh what a view!
His friends still snickered, safe nearby,
'Next time, try another try!'

The rabbits raced to see what's there,
But tangled up, they couldn't fare.
With floppy ears and giggles loud,
They wriggled free, so very proud.

So in this realm of wood and cheer,
Every mishap brought them near.
Through pine and peaceful, funny times,
Their joy was woven into rhymes.

Whispers of the Woodland

In the wood where squirrels plot,
Acorns roll like clumsy shots.
A rabbit sneezes, all take flight,
Chasing shadows, what a sight!

The fox tells tales of midnight snacks,
While owls hoot and plot their hacks.
The raccoons dance with pots and pans,
As critters join in wild prance!

Mice wear ties, all dressed to charm,
While deer discuss the latest farm.
A hedgehog juggles acorn hats,
While frogs debate the best of spats!

So if you wander through this place,
Beware of laughter, see their grace.
The woodland whispers secrets sly,
With every rustle, giggle, and sigh.

Echoes of the Ancient Grove

In the grove, trees twist and lean,
Barking up jokes, they're quite the scene.
A squirrel wears a tiny crown,
While frogs with tambourines get down!

Branches sway with laughter loud,
As shadows form a smiling crowd.
The mice do pirouettes on leaves,
While ants discuss their comic thieves!

A wise old owl spins tales of old,
Of berry pies and treasures gold.
With each flap, the stories grow,
As giggles echo where winds blow!

The blush of berries, a splash of cheer,
Reminds us joy can thrive right here.
In this ancient grove, come and see,
The funniest things 'neath every tree!

Secrets of the Canopy

Up high where the leafy secrets dwell,
The monkeys weave their jokes quite well.
A parrot mimics with perfect flair,
As flying squirrels take to the air!

The laughter drips like morning dew,
As branches gossip how trees grew.
A beetle rolls a leaf like a ball,
While sloths outpace with a leisurely crawl!

Raccoons hold a tea party grand,
Served on leaves, oh isn't it grand?
Jellybeans are the sweets they share,
With owls raising paws in the air!

Secrets whispered from branch to bough,
In the canopy, fun's happening now.
So join the frolic, bring your cheer,
The best laughter is always near!

Beneath the Verdant Veil

Beneath the veil of emerald green,
Fluffy bunnies hop with gleam.
A turtle sings a tuneless song,
While the ants dance along all day long!

Laughter echoes through the glade,
As mushrooms watch the silly parade.
A gnome juggles with twigs and stones,
While badgers trade their funny tones!

Grasshoppers invite the crowd to feast,
On picnic spreads, gathered at least.
Beetles race in a crazy line,
While chipmunks scheme for a big cheese dine!

So stroll beneath this leafy zone,
Where humor lives in every tone.
With creatures merry, spirits bright,
Join the fun, it feels so right!

The Tryst of Twilight and Bark

In the glade where shadows play,
A squirrel wore a hat today.
He danced with glee, a merry sight,
While rabbits laughed in pure delight.

A wise old owl with glasses perched,
Told tales of grasshoppers, well-researched.
He hooted jokes, so loudly bold,
That even the shy mushrooms rolled.

Underneath the willow's sweep,
A hedgehog sang, while others sleep.
He strummed a leaf like a guitar,
And summoned critters from afar.

As dusk fell softly on the scene,
The forest filled with laughter keen.
All critters joined to sing and cheer,
For twilight's fun was finally here.

Whimsy of the Whispering Woods

In the woods where whispers bloom,
A cheeky fox popped out with zoom.
He wore a cloak of leaves and twine,
And declared himself a forest dine!

The rabbits giggled, tucked in the grass,
As Bruno the bear stumbled past.
He tripped on roots and rolled with glee,
Declared, 'This forest's fun for me!'

A bird flew by with a silly song,
While all the trees swayed along.
They chuckled leaves off every branch,
And twirled 'round in a merry dance.

At the owl's tavern, tales were spun,
Of pranks and fun for everyone.
The stars above twinkled bright,
In the whimsy of the night.

The Odyssey of Oak and Pine

Oak and Pine set out one day,
For an adventure, come what may.
They found a map that led them far,
To a treasure beneath a star!

With acorns packed and roots in tow,
They dodged a stream and danced in snow.
A passing turtle gave a grin,
And joined their quest, adding to the din.

Through bramble thick, they burrowed deep,
While squirrels yelled and cats did leap.
They stumbled upon a gnome in fright,
Who offered snacks for their delight.

The treasure turned out to be a feast,
With nuts and berries, quite the beast!
So Oak and Pine, with turtle too,
Celebrated, as new friends do.

Folktales Under the Twinkling Stars

Beneath the stars, the critters sat,
An old raccoon began like that.
With sly, bright eyes and tales galore,
He spun a yarn of yore once more.

A porcupine chimed in with flair,
About a cat with quite a dare.
He chased his tail 'til dizzy grew,
And tumbled in a muddy stew!

The fireflies flickered, adding light,
As laughter echoed through the night.
An elf in bloom joined in the song,
His tiny voice, sweet and strong.

With every tale, the night grew warm,
And friendship sparkled, safe from harm.
So under stars, they wove their dreams,
In the magic of the moonlit beams.

Flights of the Forest Spirits

In the glade where whispers twirl,
Silly spirits dance and swirl.
They trip over roots and rocks,
Wearing leaves like funny frocks.

One lost a shoe, a puny boot,
While teasing a squirrel in a suit.
They giggled loud, but oh, what woes,
For causing a fuss with their silly shows!

A wise old owl watched with delight,
As fairies flipped and took to flight.
With tattered wings and wild hair,
They spun around without a care.

At dusk they promised not to prance,
Yet just couldn't help but steal a glance.
Through twilight's mist, their giggles rang,
The forest echoed with their gang!

Eternal Echoes of Wilderness

Deep in the woods where shadows play,
Echoes of laughter lead the way.
A bear told jokes to a passing fox,
While squirrels laughed and danced in socks.

A rabbit bounced, lost in a pun,
Swinging his carrots, oh what fun!
A deer nearby rolled on the ground,
In fits of giggles, he spun around.

Old trees creaked, their voices grinned,
As breezes joined the cheerful din.
Each rustle sounded like a jest,
In nature's play, they found their zest.

Off in the distance, a wolf chimed in,
Adding his howl to the joyful din.
Together they created a funny score,
In the wilderness, forever more!

The Saga of Saplings

In the thicket where young ones grow,
Saplings plot with a lively show.
They stretch their limbs and tell tall tales,
Of brave adventures in the gales.

One shouted, "Look, I'm a mighty tree!"
While swaying gently with glee.
Another whispered, "I'll fly to the moon,"
But tripped on a vine and fell down too soon!

These playful sprouts, they dream so free,
Of paths not taken, of all they'd be.
With roots still tangled in earthy fun,
They chirp and laugh 'til day is done.

As shadows fall, their giggles rise,
The starlit skies become their prize.
In the warmth of night, they bound and twine,
Chasing the moonbeam, oh what a line!

The Moonlit Metaphor

Under the moon's soft, glowing gaze,
A band of critters spent their days.
A raccoon wearing a tiny crown,
Clumsily danced, then fell right down.

Fireflies flickered, bright and bold,
Whispering secrets, stories told.
A hedgehog giggled, "What a sight!
The moon is laughing with pure delight!"

With shadows stretched and patterns spun,
The forest humored everyone.
A cat with whiskers almost too grand,
Joined in the jest, a slapstick band.

All creatures joined in, a lively crew,
Under stars sparkling like morning dew.
Their banter echoed through the night,
In metaphor, they found pure light!

Mysteries in the Dappled Light

In shadows where the squirrels play,
A raccoon steals bonbons on his way.
The owls glare from their shady heights,
Chortling at the chipmunk's silly flights.

Beneath the leaves, old mysteries dwell,
Like why the frogs sing so well.
A turtle's joke brings giggles anew,
While ants form a line for a tasty stew.

Each rustle tells a tale of fun,
Of ladybugs racing 'til the day is done.
The trees whisper secrets through the breeze,
As everyone mulls over bugs and fees.

Yet as the sun begins to fall,
A fox in a hat gives it his all.
He tips his cap, with a wink and a grin,
Inviting all to join in his din.

A Serenade for the Silent Ones

In quiet corners, crickets play,
While owls hoot in a jazzy way.
The hedgehogs sway, all dressed in spikes,
Dropping tunes like small, quirky hikes.

Behind tall ferns the rabbits chatter,
With puns about the squirrels' scatter.
The mushrooms giggle, their laughter loud,
Encouraging a dance from every shroud.

A snail with shades glides slowly through,
Sipping dew drops, feeling brand new.
His friends cheer on in rhythmic style,
As laughter stretches for another mile.

And when the stars peek through the trees,
The night comes alive with fantastic bees.
With twirls and jumps, they laugh and sing,
Imagining themselves as the woodland king.

Songs of the Oldest Pines

Under ancient boughs, the secrets spin,
Where shadows meet and laughter begins.
The mossy rocks play a steady beat,
While creatures clap with tiny feet.

The eldest pine sways and bends,
Telling tales of old, to quite a few friends.
A raccoon in pjs wiggles with glee,
As he juggles acorns beneath a tree.

With each gust of wind, a chorus of sound,
As branches creak and leaves dance around.
The woodpeckers drum on a tree like a game,
Turning the woods into a wild fame.

At twilight, a party in full swing,
Where the shadows join in like they're a thing.
Each twig snaps with joy, each root starts to sway,
In this wooden world where fun never strays.

The Dance of the Dusk Creatures

As the sun dips low, the critters emerge,
Bouncing and leaping with a joyful surge.
Fireflies twirl in their evening waltz,
While badgers chatter, ignoring their faults.

A hedgehog spins, looking suave with flair,
Wearing a leaf crown, without a care.
The shadows giggle, playing peek-a-boo,
As a wily fox pulls off antics too.

With acorn hats, they gather around,
As nightingale choirs harmonize sound.
Even the trees sway to the fun,
Welcoming the antics until they're done.

So dance through the dusk 'neath the starry sheen,
Where laughter echoes, and joy is keen.
In this wild world, the night sings loud,
As dusk creatures shimmy and dance all proud.

Glittering Glades and Gnarled Branches

In a glade where rabbits prance,
Squirrels perform a silly dance,
Trees wear hats made from old shoes,
While birds gossip about the news.

A turtle races, moving slow,
While frogs cheer for their absent bro,
The flowers giggle in the sun,
As raccoons plot their next big run.

A wise old owl gives quirky tips,
While mushrooms join in on the flips,
The laughter echoes, wild and free,
In this land of glee and mystery.

All creatures sing a joyful tune,
Beneath the watchful gaze of the moon,
In these woods, where fun abounds,
A magical world, where joy resounds.

Reverberations of the Rustic Realm

In the woods where laughter flows,
A weasel wears a silly nose,
The trees chuckle, branches sway,
As critters join this grand ballet.

A bear attempts to ride a bike,
While squirrels joke, "He'll take a hike!"
A family of ducks waddle by,
In hats and shades, oh my, oh my!

The mushrooms dance in polka dots,
While beetles spin in fancy knots,
The brook hums with a merry tune,
Beneath the bright, and happy moon.

From funny tales of squirrels bold,
To dancing bugs with hearts of gold,
This rustic realm, where dreams ignite,
Brings heaps of laughter through the night.

The Color of Twilight in the Woods

At twilight's brush, the mischief starts,
With glowworms telling silly arts,
The trees, adorned in glitter bright,
Join woodland creatures in their flight.

A hedgehog dons a tiny crown,
As crickets play a merry frown,
Fireflies twinkle like small stars,
While chipmunks play on old guitars.

A fox thinks he can sing a tune,
But ends up yowling at the moon,
The laughter spreads from leaf to leaf,
In this heartwarming, joyous relief.

The twilight paints a scene so grand,
As creatures dance in merry band,
With spirits high, they roam and play,
In the vibrant colors of the day.

The Chronicles of Charmed Groves

In enchanted groves where whimsy flows,
The berries gossip, and the wind blows,
A dancing fox with shoes so bright,
Steals the show from the moonlit night.

An owl trades secrets with the trees,
While rabbits giggle in the breeze,
A hedgehog reads a tale so grand,
With mushrooms gathered hand in hand.

A band of ants begins to play,
While crickets keep the beat all day,
The sun winks down, a warm embrace,
As all the creatures find their place.

With every turn, a laugh or cheer,
In this grove, there's naught to fear,
For in this world, of frolic and jest,
The tales unfold of merriest quest.

The Language of Leaves

In the trees, the whispers flow,
Leaves gossip softly, don't you know?
A pine told a tale of a squirrel's feast,
While oak laughed hard at the elm's new least.

Each rustle and crack, a punchline shared,
In this leafy world, all woes are bared.
The breeze giggles through branches above,
Nature's own stand-up, a show full of love.

Murmurs in the Wilderness

Foxes debate over who runs the best,
While snails race slow, they just can't jest.
A rabbit in bowtie, so dapper and spry,
Cracks jokes to the frogs while they leap and sigh.

The shadows dance, squirrels do prance,
As crickets chirp in a rhythmic chance.
Each critter laughs, a silly brigade,
In the wild, nothing is ever delayed.

The Woodland's Enchantment

Mushrooms wear hats, so vibrant and round,
Holding a party on soft, mossy ground.
A hedgehog served cake, though spiky his style,
And told a corny joke that made everyone smile.

Bouncing from bramble to tree trunk they race,
While owls hoot their cheer in this happy place.
A chipmunk's tune makes the night shift and sway,
In this magical land, laughter leads the way.

Echoes of the Elder Trees

Old trees share tales in creaky old voices,
Of raucous raccoons and unwise choices.
A woodpecker's knock is a drumstick's call,
As crickets chime in, a concert for all.

The squirrels debate who buries the best,
While hedgehogs nap, dreaming of quests.
When night falls near, the giggles ignite,
In the shadows of giants, it feels just right.

Woven in Wilderness

In a forest of chatter, the squirrels convene,
Planning a heist for some nuts quite unseen.
A raccoon with swagger, a trader of gear,
Sells shiny odd trinkets, with laughter and cheer.

A wise old owl acts, as the judge of their games,
Calls out a winner, but forgets all their names.
The trees shake with giggles, branches twist in glee,
As rabbits join in, all too clever to flee.

The Ethereal Pathway

On a path made of moss, the fairies parade,
In sandals of dew, with sunlight arrayed.
They dance with the shadows, twirl with delight,
While a hedgehog looks on, in astonished fright.

A fox in a top hat, with a cane made of bark,
Claims that he's royalty, he's quite a lark!
But when he trips over, the vines by the stream,
The giggles erupt—it's a ridiculous dream.

Roots of the Ancient Trees

Beneath the thick canopy, the roots twist and sprawl,
They whisper of secrets, of creatures so small.
A turtle in glasses recites ancient lore,
While the ants take a vote on their snack from the store.

A nest full of robins, all vying for fame,
Hatch plans for a concert—a dazzling game.
But the wind plays a trick, and the notes go astray,
With a cacophony echoing, all run away!

The Talk of Treetops

Up high in the branches, the crows hold a chat,
Discussing the antics of a cheeky old cat.
With beaks full of gossip, they squawk and they caw,
About who stole whom's lunch—oh what a great flaw!

A squirrel swings by, in a cape made of leaves,
Proclaiming his heroics, "I've rescued the bees!"
But alas, in his haste, he trips on thin air,
Creating a tumble—a spectacular flare!

Nature's Poetic Canvas

In the woods where squirrels dance,
Frogs in tuxedos take a chance.
Leaves flicker like a paintbrush bright,
Every critter's a poet, taking flight.

Breezes tickle the trees up high,
While owl chefs bake pies with a sigh.
The mischievous raccoons sing and tease,
As the chipmunks play hopscotch with ease.

Mushrooms form a jovial crowd,
Telling jokes, oh, they're quite loud!
The sun winks through branches in jest,
Nature's laughter, simply the best!

Colors splash like a painter's spree,
In this park full of jubilee.
Each creature a jester, each sound a rhyme,
A rollicking ode lost in time.

The Heartbeat of Hollowed Logs

Underneath an ancient oak,
Squirrels gather, sharing a joke.
Rabbits hop with a cheeky grin,
While badgers gamble for a win.

Logs that thump with a silly beat,
Dance with ants on wiggly feet.
Mice juggle acorns, quite the show,
While woodpeckers drum with a flair to grow.

Fungi sprout, wearing silly hats,
A parade of colors, where laughter chats.
The bees hum tunes of sweet delight,
As fireflies join in, sparkling bright.

Echoing giggles in the cool night air,
Creatures revel without a care.
Nature's party, a splendid sight,
In hollowed logs, the joy ignites.

Fables from the Fern-filled Valley

In a valley lush with springy ferns,
The wise old toad with stories turns.
Tales of ducks and a chicken dance,
Where mischief brews, and critters prance.

Badgers run with socks askew,
While frogs debate who's best in blue.
A hedgehog's spiky haircut shock,
Takes the stage on a mossy rock.

An otter slips, gives a happy shout,
While the wise trees laugh and twist about.
Their roots, like storytellers, share,
Fables that bring joy everywhere.

As night falls, they boast and cheer,
In this valley, laughter's clear.
Nature's tales under a starry quilt,
In every giggle, the world is built.

The Song of the Selkie's Stream

Down by the stream where mermaids hide,
A selkie sings, with fishes beside.
Turtles float by wearing tiny caps,
As butterflies dance in gentle laps.

With splashes and giggles, the otters glide,
While frogs with banjos sit side by side.
The water sparkles with laughter sweet,
As feisty minnows tap their feet.

Upstream there's a party, crabs in line,
Marshmallows toast, everything's fine.
Hare on the flute plays a tune so bright,
While snakes shake tails, oh what a sight!

A shimmering moon starts to softly gleam,
As creatures gather, lost in the dream.
The selkie whispers, "Let's sing once more,"
In this joyous place that we all adore.

A Tapestry of Tranquility

In the woods, a squirrel laughs,
With acorn hats and tiny staffs.
A rabbit hops, a dance so spry,
While butterflies just float on by.

Mushrooms grin from every side,
As lizards wear their coats of pride.
The trees all whisper silly dreams,
Of twigs that play in flowing streams.

A hedgehog juggles twigs with glee,
While birds compose a symphony.
The sun beams down, a spotlight bright,
On woodland antics, pure delight.

Nightfall comes, the critters yawn,
The dance of day now gently gone.
With giggles soft, they find their beds,
In leafy homes, with dreams in heads.

The Dance of the Dappled Glade

In dappled light, the foxes prance,
With their friends, they take a chance.
They flip and flop, a funny sight,
Creating laughs till the night.

A raccoon dons a silly mask,
Pretending to be quite the task.
The owls hoot jokes from their trees,
While bushes shake with merry ease.

The bees form bands, with buzzing tunes,
As squirrel plays the tambourines.
The fawns try their first wobbly spins,
While frogs just croak about their wins.

As stars poke through the leafy maze,
The night is filled with fun and plays.
And all together, they declare,
Tomorrow brings more tales to share!

Chronicles of the Woodland Spirits

In the glen, the spirits gleam,
With playful charms and giggling dreams.
A sprite named Pip starts a prank,
Turning acorns to a tiny tank.

The gnomes conspire, plotting their tricks,
While hedgehogs roll in funny flicks.
Each bush is filled with hidden laughs,
As butterflies sprout tiny staffs.

The wise old owl spots a joke,
He ruffles feathers, eyes a poke.
With cackles loud, the winds do swirl,
As mushrooms twirl in a silly whirl.

When day wraps up in soft moonlight,
The woodland squad bids joy goodnight.
In dreams they dance, in jest they play,
A nightly feast of fun and fray.

Secrets of the Shaded Realm

In shadowed nooks, the secrets breathe,
A dancing vine, a laughing sheathe.
With squirrels telling tales of cheese,
And ferns that sway, as if to tease.

In cozy corners, buzzing flies,
Conduct a show beneath the skies.
A badger sings with mighty might,
While crickets join the serenade night.

The oak tree leans to share a jest,
While chipmunks suit up, looking best.
With twinkling eyes and wiggly tails,
They share the giggles as joy prevails.

As twilight falls, the jokes unwind,
In this realm that's sweetly kind.
The whispers fade, but laughter swells,
In woods that guard their fun-filled spells.

Dreams in the Aromatic Aisles

In the grove where mushrooms dance,
Squirrels wear hats and prance.
They argue who eats more nuts,
While the wise old owl just mutts.

Flowers giggle in the breeze,
Sharing secrets with the trees.
They tease the bugs that pass by,
Trying to soar, yet always shy.

Ladybugs try to keep score,
While ants rush past for the door.
Tadpoles toast with cups of dew,
A little party, just for two.

As twilight falls, the shadows play,
Frogs recite their rhyming sway.
In this aisle of whimsy and cheer,
Every creature holds their beer.

The Lost Songs of the Leafy Realm

High in branches, birds once sang,
Now they just chatter and hang.
A parrot claims he's a great star,
But his talent's a bit bizarre.

Caterpillars dream of flight,
While munching leaves, they lose sight.
Their melodies are quite a rack,
But who'll tell them? That's the knack!

Twisty vines try to compose,
With discordant notes that doze.
Frogs croak softly, bringing cheer,
Their tuneful sound, we hold dear.

Yet in dusk, a chorus grows,
Crickets join in with their prose.
The leafy realm, a stage so bright,
Under stars, they find their light.

Lurking beneath the Emerald Arch

Beneath vines, a rabbit lurks,
Plotting pranks, oh what a jerk!
He hides behind a tall fern,
Waiting for his turn to churn.

A raccoon whispers rumors bold,
Of treasures lost and tales retold.
But shadows creep as night comes fast,
And laughter echoes from the past.

Mossy stones play hide and seek,
Frog leaps out, give a squeak!
His friends all dive in pure surprise,
With antics mixed, like pies in the skies.

Here among roots, mischief grows,
Each twist and turn, the joke just flows.
Beneath the arch, where secrets blend,
Every day's a quest, it won't end!

Threads of Moonlight on Mossy Paths

Through the woods where shadows twine,
Mice wear capes, looking divine.
They scamper quick, a little race,
Tripping over roots with grace.

Bats play tag in the silver glow,
While fireflies put on a show.
With giggles soft, they dip and dive,
In this space, they feel alive.

A hedgehog rolls and starts to spin,
Trying his best to win the grin.
But tumbling down is part of the fun,
As midnight whispers, "You're number one!"

With threads of light on paths so bold,
Adventures spark, tales unfold.
In every nook, a laugh is sought,
In the woods, joy can't be bought.

Whispers of the Whimsical Woods

In the woods where the squirrels plot,
A raccoon sings a tune, quite forgot.
The owl hoots puns in the moonlight,
While dancing trees sway, what a sight!

The mushrooms giggle, they seem to smirk,
As rabbits in capes dash, oh what a quirk!
A fox in glasses reads a book,
While the pine trees listen with a curious look.

The brook babbles jokes with a splash,
While butterflies laugh in a colorful flash.
And don't forget the bees with caps,
Buzzing about in playful laps!

So if you wander beneath the leaves,
Prepare for chuckles that never leave.
For in these woods of glee and cheer,
Laughter echoes, loud and clear!

Legends in the Leafy Canopy

Beneath the boughs where legends sprout,
A turtle tells tales, without a doubt.
The wily crow caws with delight,
As the hedgehog prances in full sight.

The sunbeams giggle, tickling the ferns,
While ladybugs dance with colorful turns.
Each leaf holds secrets, or so they say,
Of clumsy giants that danced in the bay.

The fruit bats joke about their flight,
Trying to soar, but landing slight.
A wisp of fog trips over the ground,
While a wise old toad croaks laughter profound.

In leafy realms where laughter reigns,
The grass sings songs with funny refrains.
So come and revel, my friend, my mate,
In these whimsical tales that we create!

Smoke and Shadows in a Woven World

In a world of smoke where shadows tease,
A rabbit brews tea beneath the trees.
The wisps of fog tickle the air,
While fireflies gossip without a care.

The toadstools gather for a big debate,
On who has the best dance, it's quite the fate!
A bear in a hat plays the spoons,
While raccoons waltz under the moon.

The fog swirls around, oh what a sight,
As squirrels recount tales of their fright.
With every puff, more laughter grows,
As shadows prance on their silly toes.

So if you wander where shadows play,
Join in the fun, don't delay!
This woven world spins a tale so bright,
Filled with giggles and pure delight!

The Harp of the Wildflowers

In fields where wildflowers strum their strings,
A dandelion chorus joyfully sings.
The petals sway, a colorful show,
As butterflies join in the lively flow.

A grasshopper hops with a tap-tap beat,
Inviting the ants for a dance on their feet.
While daisies chuckle, swaying just so,
With a breeze that whispers, 'Come on, let's go!'

Bees buzz along, in perfect harmony,
While the sunbeams dance, full of glee.
And even the thistles join in the play,
With prickly jokes that never fray.

So gather around, let your laughter soar,
Join the wildflower harp, forevermore.
In this merry bloom of color and cheer,
Every note of joy is crystal clear!

Heroines of the Shaded Halls

In leafy halls where laughter grows,
The squirrel spins tales of doggy woes.
A rabbit with glasses reads a book,
While a dancing mouse takes on the cook.

The mushrooms giggle, they can't keep straight,
As snails prepare for a racing fate.
With crowns of flowers, the critters prance,
In their woodland ball, they twirl and dance.

Footsteps in the Ferns

Footsteps puff through the vibrant greens,
A hedgehog huffs, 'I need more beans!'
While butterflies flit on a keen diet,
The ants form a band, oh what a riot!

With each crunch, the ferns beam bright,
As everyone dons their fancy flight.
'Tis a party here in the foliage land,
With laughter and games all perfectly planned.

Phantoms of the Canopy Murmurs

A ghostly owl hoots a tune,
While raccoons waltz under the moon.
The shadows giggle, they're playing tricks,
With acorns flying like magic flicks.

The trees whisper secrets in playful glee,
While a clumsy fox spills his herbal tea.
Mistaken identities lead to surprise,
As everyone laughs with wide-open eyes.

Threads of Life in the Leafy Labyrinth

In a maze of greens with twists and turns,
The wise old tortoise patiently learns.
While chipmunks plot a nutty heist,
Their giggles echo like a merry feast.

Through tangled paths and hidden trails,
The sparrows chirp of their grand tales.
With twigs for swords and leaves for capes,
The laughter bubbles as nature shapes.

Chronicles of the Canopy's Heart

In a tree with legs, a squirrel danced,
Chasing after acorns, he pranced.
A wise old owl, with glasses on,
Gave lectures on how to lure a con.

The raccoon baked cookies, oh what a sight,
In his little kitchen, all through the night.
But with sticky paws, he stole his own treat,
And ran in a panic, with crumbs on his feet.

A mischievous crow, with a jest in the air,
Told a joke to the leaves, who just didn't care.
As the branches giggled, the sun had a laugh,
From the tiniest fern to the grandest giraffe.

At twilight's glow, the creatures all cheered,
For the tales of the trees, which nobody feared.
In this whimsical realm, joy takes the lead,
With laughter and folly, fulfilling each need.

When the Wild Whispers

A fox with a hat tripped over a log,
Mumbling to himself, what a silly dog!
The rabbits all snickered, their giggles in tune,
As the fox borrowed shoes, to dance 'neath the moon.

A bear in bright socks, who loved to disco,
Twisted and twirled, oh what a show!
With each playful stumble, and each little spin,
He rolled in the grass, with a laugh and a grin.

The glen filled with sounds, mischievous and loud,
As a tortoise rapped, saying, "I'm slow but proud!"
The critters all bobbed, their tails a-twirling,
As the stars overhead began softly swirling.

In a meadow so bright, the party took flight,
With friends from the trees, all sharing delight.
A chorus of chuckles, they found such great fun,
And the wild whispered tales, until day was done.

Secrets Carved in the Earth

Beneath the green roots, a secret was spun,
A worm dreamed of cake, oh what a fun run!
With sprinkles of soil, and frosting of dew,
He hosted a party for ants, who just flew.

A mole with a map, claimed treasures below,
Finding lost keys to a world they did know.
With giggles erupting, they dug and they found,
A hat made of leaves and a violin sound.

Squirrels held signs like, "Here to perform!"
While rabbits provided a cheerleading swarm.
The night was a ruckus of joy under stars,
With dance-offs and riddles beneath the moon's bars.

From whispers of roots, to skies full of glee,
These secrets of earth made all creatures agree.
In laughter they shared, and in fun, they believed,
That every odd moment is meant to be weaved.

The Legacy of Lush Landscapes

In patches of green, lived a cow with a dream,
To juggle fresh apples while sipping on cream.
But she wobbled and fumbled, much to her despair,
As the apples all tumbled, into the air!

A parrot, quite clever, made copies of tunes,
Sang songs of the soil to swooning raccoons.
While together they giggled at the cows' grand endeavor,
Turning fails into tales, oh, it made them clever!

A deer in a tutu pirouetted with flair,
While frogs clapped and croaked, in the warm evening air.

As laughter erupted, the trees swayed with glee,
In a circus of antics, where wildness ran free.

With each landscape lush, and mischief so bright,
The legacy lived on, as stars filled the night.
So in every last corner, where joy finds its way,
These moments of wildness forever will stay.

Conversations with the Elder Trees

I asked the oak for life tips today,
He chuckled, 'Just let the wind play!'
The willow swayed with grace and delight,
Said, 'Dance with shadows, stay out of sight!'

The birch chimed in, 'Don't take it too hard,
Life's just a game, discard the old card!'
With laughter echoing, the forest did gleam,
A council of trees, plotting a dream.

Guardians of the Whispering Woods

In the woods where whispers do dwell,
The guardians gather, casting their spell.
With mischievous grins, they play tricks in the night,
Turning lost hikers into giggling fright!

A squirrel named Chuck claimed the tree as his throne,
'You'll never escape, you're stuck in my zone!'
With acorns of laughter tossed overhead,
They echoed the nonsense, as night gently bled.

Spirits of the Submerged Roots

Beneath the green, where the muddy roots lie,
Spirits of mischief catch fish passing by.
With splashes and giggles, they'd tickle and tease,
The fish couldn't swim, they just floated with ease!

The spirits would hide, play games of charades,
As frogs joined the fun in their slippery parades.
Laughing and croaking, they'd sing through the muck,
A party ensues, nothing's ever amuck!

Love Letters to the Wildflowers

Sweet daisies giggle, teasing the bees,
'It's a flower's world, swoop down, if you please!'
The roses, they blushed, with petals so bright,
'Write us some love notes under the moonlight!'

With sunlit confessions and breezy warm sighs,
The wildflowers bloom, sharing secrets and lies.
Each stalk stands tall with a quirky romance,
As petals twirl gently in a whimsical dance.

Tales from the Sylvan Shadows

In the woodlands, where squirrels conspire,
A tree could talk, it would surely retire.
The owls teach jokes that are quite a hoot,
While rabbits wear socks with flour on their foot.

The hedgehogs compete in a race with the snails,
But the winner is always the one with the tales.
Mice hold a banquet of cheese and of wine,
They toast to the trees and declare them divine.

A deer struts by, sporting sunglasses so cool,
While chipmunks play cards in a makeshift school.
The fox tells a story so woven with lies,
That even the trees roll their big ancient eyes.

So gather 'round, friends, with your laughter and cheer,
In the forest of fun, there's nothing to fear.
With shadows that dance and the sunlight that glows,
You'll find the wild tales that the woodland bestows.

Chronicles of the Timbered Realm

Once a tree claimed it could sing like a bird,
But when it opened its mouth, not a sound was heard.
The squirrels laughed loud, and the raccoons sneered,
Oh, the jokes in the woods are the best, it's cleared!

A worm with a bow tie made quite the scene,
He ran for mayor, with hopes that were keen.
His platform was juice—apple, grape, and pear!
But the ants voted back, "You're hardly a player!"

The hedgehog is known as quite the wise sage,
With anecdotes shared from a very old page.
When asked for advice, he just chuckles and grins,
"Less thorns in your side, and more room for your sins!"

But all in good jest, as the forest abounds,
With whispers of laughter where joy can be found.
In timbered retreats, let your spirits take flight,
For the chronicles here, are a sheer pure delight!

The Enchanted Glade's Lament

An acorn once dreamed of being a tree,
But it quipped with a laugh, "I'll be wild and free!"
The mushrooms just giggled, they couldn't contain,
As the wind whispered softly, "You'll grow in great pain."

A toad with a crown sat high on a rock,
He ruled over bugs, and he tickled the clock.
"Let's dance, little friends, till the moon hits the ground,
For laughter's our treasure where true joy is found!"

The willows sway gently, their branches with glee,
As gossiping squirrels debate who's the "he."
They mutter and mutter, all through the night,
With stories convoluted and hearts shining bright.

Yet the glade knows well, despite all the jest,
That laughter and folly are truly the best.
For in every chuckle, and every wise crack,
Connects all the critters to share in the laugh!

Breezes of the Bark-clad Beacons

In a glade that's alive with chatter and peace,
A woodpecker knocks, giving laughter release.
While bees buzz along, making syllables rhyme,
For the barks of the trees all echo in time.

A porcupine dressed in a tuxedo so fine,
Slips on some old leaves for a dance by design.
His partners, the shrews, whirl with giggles and spins,
Their tiny hearts soaring, embracing their wins.

The owls, too cool, with shades on their beaks,
Share riddles at midnight; they giggle and squeak.
The fireflies twinkle, like fairies in flight,
Painting the night sky with sparkles of light.

So when you're amidst the bark-clad retreats,
Join in on the fun where adventure repeats.
For laughter's the language that echoes with grace,
In the breezes that dance through this magical place.

www.ingramcontent.com/pod-product-compliance
Lightning Source LLC
Chambersburg PA
CBHW051646160426
43209CB00004B/806